When Mama was as young [...] metro didn't go to the b[...] was no beach like there i[...] there. It sounds strange [...] but not that old. She is not a grandmother, let alone a great-grandmother. And yet, she knew a city closed to the sea, where people had to take the train or the Seat 600 (a classic car from that era, as round as a snail) to go for a dip or to sunbathe. Luckily the Olympic Games in 1992 gave the excuse to make the city prettier. The athletes won medals and Barcelona won the sea in which my siblings and I bathe every summer. Only six metro stations separate our house from the Vila Olimpica station: we can reach the waves in ten minutes.

My sister is doing a school research paper on the history of Barcelona and she has asked me to help her write it. Aina is the eldest of us four siblings and the only girl. I am neither the eldest nor the youngest, and I am not even the only middle one. My name is Abel and I am ten years old. Aina was born three years after the Olympics, when the athletes' medals still shone. This week, the first of the summer holidays, she and I will walk wide-eyed around the city where we were born. I am looking forward to being a tourist without leaving home. Without leaving Barcelona, I mean.

As today is Monday, we have to go to Ciutat Vella. Aina has decided that we must begin in the middle, to know where we come from. I told her it's like starting a peach from the pit, and that we both come from the belly of the same mother, but I don't think she found it funny. And here we are taking the metro to Jaume I, which is where we go every 5th January to watch the parade of the Three Wise Men.

The Romans came here over two hundred years before Christ was born and founded the city of Barcino on Mount Tàber, right where we are now, between the cathedral and Plaça Sant Jaume. The city was surrounded by walls, with four entrance gates. In Plaça Ramon Berenguer, close to the Gothic cathedral, there are still remains of the wall. And under the Plaça del Rei lie the remains of the heart of the Roman city. It is impressive that these stones are so old. I was going to say that it makes me a little jealous because people don't live that many years, but I won't say anything: being a stone must be very boring. The truth is that I would stop looking at stones and go to look at paintings in the Museu Picasso, which is in Montcada Street, five minutes from here, but it is closed on Mondays. What a pity.

PARLAMENT DE
1716-1748

PARLAMENT DE CATALUNYA

ZOO

BCN

AJUNTAMENT DE BARCELONA 1847

The people who govern in Barcelona are mainly based in Plaça Sant Jaume. Well, not all of them: there is the Parliament in Ciutadella Park, next to the zoo, where the deputies work (they work in the Parliament, not with the animals!). But in this square the Catalonian Generalitat faces the Barcelona Council. The president of the Catalan government has his office in the Generalitat and the mayor has his in the Council building. Maybe some mornings, the two coincide in the square and greet each other or they have breakfast together in that place where they make really good sandwiches and there's always a queue. And who knows if at Christmas they escape for a moment to look at the nativity scene which is set up in the square every year. A tradition which is preserved even though in Barcelona there are people of all religions and other people who do not need religion to live.

I like to walk through the centre. In ancient times, Plaça Catalunya was a field outside the city walls. It is very big and there are a lot of pigeons. Mama says that when she was a child there were even more, but perhaps that is a trick of memory. The square, which is named after the country, often hosts concerts. Today, Tuesday, Aina has arranged to meet a friend right in the middle of the square. Mireia want to join us to cross the most entertaining, most surprising and fullest street in the city: the Rambla. It goes from Plaça Catalunya to the port. Aina has asked me to hold her hand. She is worried I will get lost. I said I am not Aniol, our little brother. But I do what she says because I do not want to get lost.

At the Canaletes fountain, they celebrate Barça victories. Before 1860, there wasn't a wrought iron fountain, but a pump from which they say the freshest and purest water in the city came. Today they still say that tourists who drink the magic water from the fountain will return to Barcelona sooner or later. I am not a tourist, I was born in the neighbourhood of Gràcia, but I have a good drink now to quench my thirst. What a lot of people there are on the Rambla! Most are in short sleeves and shorts because it is hot. But there are even more people on 23rd April, Saint George's Day, when the whole city is filled with stalls selling books and roses. It's a day more magical than the Canaletes' water. If you come to Barcelona on Saint George's, you will fall in love with the city so much that you are sure to return.

When I was little, the Rambla had stalls with flowers and birds. Today there are stalls of all kinds, but the pets are gone. The current Rambla began to take shape when the city walls were demolished in the mid-nineteenth century. What until then had been the Malla stream became an avenue. In 1847 the Liceo theatre opened at number 51 on the Rambla. To the right is the Raval neighbourhood where all

the colours of the world are concentrated in a few streets. Further up on the same side is the Boqueria market, where my parents shop on days when they have guests. "Come on, Abel, at this rate we'll reach the Boqueria at dinnertime!" exclaims my sister. I can't help it; I get distracted watching the crowd walking up and down. A man dressed as a pirate with one eye covered has walked past. And a group of castellers, who build human towers. And a girl walking on stilts. And a grandfather with such a wrinkled face that I bet you anything that he is the oldest man in the world. And a mime who cries tears of silver paper. And a lot of people who miss the show because they have their heads down, looking at their mobiles, like Aina and my parents do. Older people are strange. Some wouldn't even look up if pigs were flying in the sky.

Now a man passes me dressed as Christopher Columbus, who discovered America almost by accident when he was trying to go to the Indies. I half look at him while I seek out the real statue on the monument to Columbus, which can be found at the end of the Rambla, pointing to the sea with his forefinger. It was built for the 1888 International Exhibition, as were the Arc del Triomf and the Born market. This bronze Columbus is on top of a sixty-metre tall iron column. High enough for the people walking on the Rambla to look like ants.

EXPOSICIO UNIVERSAL BARCELONA 1888

GOLONDRINA

Wednesday. The Gaudí route awaits us. Park Güell, the Sagrada Família, the Pedrera and Casa Batlló, in that order. This architect was amazing: he created so many houses and things. And we still have to see the Palau Güell, the Casa Vicens, the Casa Calvet, the streetlamps in the Plaça Reial and in the Pla de Palau, the gate of the Finca Miralles, Bellesguard and other architectural gems scattered throughout the city. We will start at the top in the morning and work our way down, although I could quite happily stay in Park Güell all day. It is a treasure of a park, starting with the lizard covered in pieces of ceramic tiles and continuing on to the undulating bench in the square. I say quietly to my sister that this bench reminds me of a snake and instead of telling me I'm weird, she explains that yes, the bench is often compared to a snake basking in the Mediterranean sun. On top of the lizard and below the snake, there is a space with eighty-six columns, which make me want to play hide and seek. Within the park is the Gaudí House-Museum, where the architect Antoni Gaudí lived until shortly before his death when he was hit by a tram in 1926. Every day he walked down from this house to the Sagrada Família, which is what we are going to do today.

FINCA MIRALLES

Bellesguard

In the Sagrada Família there are towers and cranes. The towers will stay forever, the cranes for the duration of the works. The temple, inspired by Gothic and Modernist styles, is impressive. Cameras work overtime. Construction began in 1882 and when it is finished, if it is ever finished, even my little brother will be old. Inside, the Sagrada Família looks like a forest. Gaudí was unique in linking architecture and nature. Just look at the Pedrera: from the outside it looks like the sea. And on the roof there are chimneys in the form of warriors. We have come from the Sagrada Família to the Pedrera by metro, and now we will go down Passeig de Gràcia to the Casa Batlló, a building they say represents the legend of Saint George, with dragon scales included.

Another great Catalan was Joan Miró. Today is Thursday and we have started in the Escorxador Park to see the Miró sculpture *Woman and Bird*. Then we take a tour of Montjuïc Mountain, where the Miró Foundation is located. We take the cable car to reach the castle (no witches or ghosts, but it is a castle). The National Palace awaits us on Montjuïc too, built for the 1929 International Exhibition. There is also the Magic Fountain, and the Greek Theatre, and major sports facilities such as the Palau Sant Jordi and the Lluis Companys Stadium, which also dates back to 1929 but was re-modelled for the 1992 Games. Years ago Montjuïc also had an amusement park, but now the only amusement park in Barcelona is located on another of the city's mountains, Tibidabo. The four of us will go tomorrow, for Aina and her research. I can't wait to get on the roller coaster. And the Talaia, which opened in 1921 and lets you see Barcelona from 550 meters above sea level. Wow!

From the viewpoints on Tibidabo, the grid of streets in the Eixample neighbourhood can be seen. It was designed by Ildefons Cerdà in 1859, after they demolished the city walls. We can also clearly distinguish a wider street, which is the Passeig de Gràcia, with the Pedrera, Casa Batlló, other modernist buildings and lots of elegant shops. This avenue combines ancient Barcelona with the former town of Gràcia, which was independent until 1897. Gràcia is a charming neighbourhood with some very interesting inhabitants. Horta, Sants and many other neighbourhoods also have lots of character, but I don't know them as well because I don't live there. In August in Gràcia there is an incredible local festival, with a street decoration contest. It's like a prelude to the big festival in Barcelona, La Mercè, which arrives in September and has an endless schedule of events. I never miss the human tower day with the *castellers*, or the dance of the giants, or the fire run, or the fireworks display with music. In fact, I don't miss anything.

In Gràcia there are so many squares that it is easy to get them confused. The Plaça del Diamant was used to name one of the great novels of Catalan literature, written by Mercè Rodoreda. In the Plaça de la Vila there is a bell tower built by the architect Antoni Rovira i Trias between 1862 and 1864. This man gives his name to another neighbourhood square, the Plaça Rovira. What most gives the feeling of being in a small town is the Plaça de la Virreina, where the Sant Joan church can be found. Having an orange juice or chocolate milk in one of the Virreina terraces, nobody would guess that they were in a large European capital city.

We will spend this weekend by the Mediterranean Sea. Here I am with my older siblings, Aina and Nil, just below the twin towers, two skyscrapers that are the gateway to the sporting marina area. The Olympic Village in Poble Nou is a neighbourhood which came to life in 1992 thanks to the famous Games. Flats were built to house the athletes. My mother's father was born and raised in one of the old flats which were demolished to build new homes. It's funny, my grandfather lived near the beach, but at that time it seemed that the sea was a hindrance rather than an asset. Luckily things changed, and now we have a city open to the sea.

Walking (my siblings) and skating (me) along the Passeig Marítim, we go from the Olympic Port to Barceloneta, a former fishing village with a fish restaurant every two paces. When we reach the old port, I put on a good-boy face and ask them to take me to visit the Aquarium: "Go on, please, then we can see fish more alive than the ones in the restaurants!" Aina and Nil laugh, but they tell me we won't have time today. "There are more days than fish in the sea, Abel!"

The Olympic Port has been here for a very short time, while the port that has been here forever has, in fact, not been here forever, but nearly: it is from the fifteenth century. Cities are made and remade throughout history. They never die and are constantly reborn. And I, who have been here for little more than ten years, I feel like a duck in water in the city where I live. I can't begin to imagine, for example, a Barcelona without beaches. They are great for swimming, making sand castles and daydreaming looking at the horizon.

I look at the line where the sea ends and I think that Catalonia is a small country, but the world is a very large ball. To the north and south, inland and beyond the Mediterranean, there are many people to meet and many cities to discover. It would be a coincidence if Barcelona were the best city in the world. But ... who knows?

# Crochet
# Designs

# Crochet
# Designs

*25 must-have items to make*

**Tess Dawson**

GUILD OF MASTER
CRAFTSMAN PUBLICATIONS

First published 2007 by
Guild of Master Craftsman
Publications Ltd, 166 High Street,
Lewes, East Sussex BN7 1XU

Reprinted 2008

ISBN 978-1-86108-434-7
A catalogue record of this book is
available from the British Library.

Photographic acknowledgements on
page 125

Production Manager: Jim Bulley
Managing Editor: Gerrie Purcell
Editor: Rachel Netherwood
Managing Art Editor: Gilda Pacitti
Design: Chloë Alexander
Photography: Jerry Lebens
Additional Photography:
Anthony Bailey

Typefaces: ITC Galliard and TheSans

Colour origination: Wyndeham
Graphics
Cover colour origination: Altaimage
Printed and bound: Sino Publishing

## Measurements notice

Imperial measurements are
conversions from metric; they have
been rounded up or down to the
nearest $\frac{1}{4}$, $\frac{1}{2}$ or whole inch.
When following the projects, use
either the metric or the imperial
measurements; do not mix units.

# Contents

# Introduction

I AM A FIDGET. There, I've admitted it now! Crochet has kept my friends and family sane as I don't fidget when I crochet so it's probably saved my hide a few times.

I got my first set of hooks from my Aunty Mina, who taught me how to crochet as a little girl growing up in Malaysia. I made clothes for my teddies and dolls, as toy shops were thin on the ground back then, and went on to make bigger things for myself and friends as I grew older. It is therapy to me in a crazy world.

Crochet is so simple to do once you have mastered the basic stitches. It's quicker than knitting (wonderful, if, like me you have the concentration span of a flea), you need fewer tools and you can't drop so many stitches if you drop your hook by accident, so it is perfect for putting down and picking up later.

You can produce solid, textured and lacy fabrics, examples of which are demonstrated in this book. Crochet is not just about granny squares and doilies – their importance is not to be sniffed at; many homes are lovingly filled with afghans and doilies – but there is so much more.

The trend for lacy crochet garments spurred me on to design a range of fashionable and quick projects, none of which are huge or too daunting so you can spend a little more money on getting a really yummy yarn and treat yourself to a little luxury.

*Jess Dawson*
x

# Scarves

Scarves are great projects
for beginners.

You can practise
different stitch techniques
to make a fast and fun
finished item.

# Blossom

*Stun your friends with this fast and easy-to-make scarf*

## Tension

12 chain sts over 4in (10cm)

## Materials

• 2 x 50g balls Angel yarns 100% Angora DK or other similar DK yarn
• 5mm crochet hook

*Abbreviations are on page 123*

## Pattern

**Row 1:** Ch 220, turn.

**Row 2:** Ch 3 and tr 1 into first st, tr 2 into every stitch until you reach the end, turn.

**Row 3:** Ch 3 and tr 1 into every st for the whole row, turn.

**Row 4:** Repeat row 2, cast off.

**To finish:** Weave in the ends.

## Note

You can make the scarf wider by adding an extra row of tr 1 into every st.

# Poppy

*This delicate scarf is a great introduction to lacework*

## Tension

11 chain sts over 4in (10cm)

## Materials

• 1 x 50g ball Rowan Kidsilk Haze, Kidsilk Night or Kidsilk Spray or other similar, lace-weight yarn
• 5mm crochet hook

*Abbreviations are on page 123*

## Pattern

**Row 1:** Ch 200, turn.

**Row 2:** Ch 4 and sl st to 5th chain from hook. Ch 4 and sl st to 2nd chain along, repeat until you reach the end of the row, turn.

**Row 3:** Ch 3 and tr 4 into the first loop made in row 2. Tr 4 into the next loop and carry on until you reach the end of this row, turn.

**Row 4:** Ch 6 and sl st to the sp between the first and 2nd fans made in the previous row, repeat this, linking to the spaces in between the fans until you reach the end of the row, turn.

**Row 5:** Ch 2 and tr 6 into the loop made in the previous row. Continue to tr 6 into each loop till you reach the end of the row, turn.

**Row 6:** Ch 4 and sl st back into the top of the last st from row 5 to form a little bobble.

*Ch 8 and sl st back to the 4th chain from hook to form a little bobble, ch 4 and sl st into the sp between the first and 2nd fan from the previous row. Ch 4 and sl st back into the same sp again to form another bobble*.

Repeat from * to * until you reach the end of the row, you will make the last bobble and sl st it to the last st from the previous row.

**To finish:** Fasten off and weave in the ends.

# Ivy

*This funky scarf is made up of individual flower motifs*

## Tension

One flower motif should be 7 ½ in (19cm) from tip to tip.

## Materials

• 2 x 100g hanks Angel yarns Seraph Alpaca or other chunky soft yarn
• 8mm crochet hook

*Abbreviations are on page 123*

## Note

The scarf is worked by making one motif at a time but joining it to the others as you go along so there is no need to stitch up the work later. This makes for a neater project as you won't have a lot of ends to weave back into the work.

## Pattern

**Row 1:** Ch 4, join with a sl st to form a circle, ch 3, tr 11 sts into the 3rd st from hook, join with a sl st to form a circle.

**Row 2:** Ch 4, join with a sl st to the tr st immediately in front of your ch, ch 4 and join with a sl st to the next st along, repeat until you reach the end of the row. You should have 12 loops in total (if you don't, you will need to unpick and go back to make sure you work 12 loops altogether).

**Row 3:** Sl st twice into the middle of the first loop so you end up at the top of the loop. *Ch 6, join with a sl st to the top of the next loop along. Ch 3, join with a sl st to the next loop*. Repeat from * to * until you reach the end of the row, linking to the first loop with a sl st.

**Row 4:** Ch 3, tr 4 into the first loop, ch 2, tr 5 down the other side of the first loop. *Join to the next little loop with 3 ch sts by working a sl st, tr 5, ch 2, tr 5 into the next loop, join with a sl st to the next little loop*. Repeat until you reach the end of the row, join to the first ch st with a sl st to complete the row.

This is your first motif; you will now work 15 more of these and join them together, after you have worked the last tr st at the top of the big star. Sl st into the point of the other star where there is a little space, then work 1 ch st and continue to work the motif. You will need to join at least 2 points on every star, with the inside stars being joined 4 times.

## Note

I have used this pattern to make a scarf but you can make anything out of this motif, such as a cushion cover or an afghan or throw for a bed or sofa. It's a great way to practise making bigger items. Keeping the points on the stars sticking out when you've finished makes it look even more pretty and lacy.

# Violet

*This snug alpaca scarf is perfect for chilly winter days*

## Tension

18 treble sts over 4in (10cm)

## Materials

• 1 x 50g ball Artesano Alpaca in Lilac (plain)
• 2 x 50g hanks of variegated Artsano Opulencia in Amethyst or other similar DK yarn
• 4.5mm crochet hook

*Abbreviations are on page 123*

## Note

This scarf is worked in two sections: the plain inside is worked first and the variegated frill is added afterwards. You can use any variation of colours for this project and any standard DK yarns can be substituted easily.

## Pattern

**Row 1:** Using the plain lilac, ch 3. The last 2 sts form the foundation first st of the 2nd row.

**Row 2:** Tr 2 into the first ch st to form a fan of 3 sts, turn. You will now increase 1 st at each end of every row until you reach 15 sts.

**Row 3:** Ch 2, tr 1 into the first and 2nd st, then tr 2 into the last st, turn (5 sts).

**Row 4:** Ch 2, tr 1 into every st except the last st where you will tr 2, turn (7 sts).

**Rows 5–8:** Repeat row 4 until you have 15 sts.

**Row 9:** Ch 2, tr 1 into every st until you get 16 sts.

**To make up:** You will now work 75 rows with these 16 sts.

Start to decrease by working 2 sts together at the start and end of each row until you have one st left. Fasten off and weave in the ends.

Join the variegated yarn to one of the pointy ends of the scarf and ch 2 to form the first st. Work a row of trebles round the outside of the whole scarf, but make sure not to overcrowd it too much – aim for a slight ruffle effect. At the end of this row, join to the first st with a sl st to finish the row.

Ch 2 and tr 2 into every st you made from row 1 to form the 2nd row. This will form a good ruffled edge round the outside of the scarf. When you reach the end of the round join to the first st with a sl st and fasten off. Weave the ends in to finish.

# Shawls

*Shawls have become the must-have accessory, adding the perfect finishing touch to any outfit.*

*This selection will suit every occasion and level of experience.*

# Indian Summer

*This pretty summer shawl
is sure to be a head turner*

## Tension

10 treble sts over 4in (10cm)

## Materials

• 8 x 50g balls Jaeger Aqua in two contrasting colours or other similar, cotton DK yarn
• 8mm crochet hook

*Abbreviations are on page 123*

## Note

You will work 1 strand of each colour together at all times. Work the semi-circle first, then work the rest of the shawl round it.

## Semi-circle pattern

**Row 1:** Ch 4, join with a sl st to form a circle.

**Row 2:** Ch 3, tr 8 into centre of circle, turn.

**Row 3:** Ch 3, tr 1 into same st. *Tr 1 into 3rd st along, ch 1, tr 1 into same st*. Repeat from * to * until you reach the end and you have 5 little triangles, turn.

**Row 4:** Ch 3, tr 1 into sp between the first and 2nd st, tr 1 into top of next st to the end (to form 21 stitches in this row), turn.

**Row 5:** Ch 3, *tr 1 into same st, tr 1 into third st along, ch 1, tr 1 into same sp again*. Repeat from * to * to the end of the row (to form 10 little triangles). Work an extra st at the end if necessary to reach the end of the row, turn.

**Row 6:** Ch 4 and join to inside sp of the next triangle along, Continue like this to the end of the row, turn.

**Row 7:** Ch 2 and tr 3 into the inside of the chain links to form a little fan of 4 st. Tr 4 into next loop and carry on until you reach the end. Turn.

**Row 8:** Repeat row 5.

**Row 9:** Repeat row 6.

**Row 10:** Repeat row 7.

**Row 11:** Ch 2 and tr 1 into every st until you reach the end, turn.

**Row 12:** Repeat row 6.

**Row 13:** Repeat row 7 and fasten off.

## Shawl pattern

Join the yarn with a sl st to one of edges of the flat sides of the semi circle and ch 39 stitches, turn. Ch 2 and tr 1 into 3rd st along , ch 1, tr 1 into same st. *Tr 1 into 3rd st along, ch 1, tr 1 into same st again* and repeat * to * until you reach the end. Join with a sl st onto the semi-circle at the same height as your tr st and sl st 2 st along the side edge of the semi-circle. Ch 1 and tr 1 back into the join you made on the last row with the semi-circle to form a little triangle.

Repeat the pattern to the end (tr 1 into 3rd st along, ch 1, tr 1 into same st again until you reach the last st) but on the last st you just tr 1 st into the end and turn. Ch 2 and carry on in pattern (tr 1 into 3rd st along, ch 1, tr 1 into same st again) until you reach the semi-circle. Work inside the brackets for these last 2 rows until you reach the top of the semi-circle. Fasten off.

Join the yarn with a sl st to the other side of the semi-circle on the other side and ch 27. Work the same as the other side, in reverse, until you reach the top of the shawl. Fasten off.

Join with a sl st to the edge of the last row and start working back and forth in pattern (tr 1 into 3rd st along, ch 1, tr 1 into same st again) until you reach the last st at the ends of the rows. Tr 1 into these last sts, turn and ch 2 to start the next row.

Continue until the end, where you should have one little triangle with a tr st left on either side. This is the point of the shawl. You will now work a border row all the way round the outside of the shawl to neaten edges. Ch 3 then work 2 tr into same st to form a fan, tr 3 times into the same sl into equal spaces along the outside edge of the shawl until you reach the beginning and fasten off.

**To finish:** Cut the tassel lengths. I wound the yarn widthways round the outside of an A4 magazine and cut both ends to make 8 ½ in (22cm) lengths but you can vary yours! Use two strands of each contrasting colour and make into tassels every 2 stitches along the bottom edges of the shawl.

# Gardenia

*This pretty shawl will add a feminine touch to any outfit*

## Tension

12 treble sts over 4in (10cm)

## Materials

• 3 x 50g balls Rowan Kidsilk Haze or other similar lace-weight yarn
• 4.5mm crochet hook

*Abbreviations are on page 123*

## Lace pattern

The pattern starts with making the lace triangle in the centre of the shawl and the ruffle edge is worked at the end.

**Row 1:** Ch 3, tr 6 into first ch space to form a fan, turn.

**Row 2:** Ch 8, sl st to 4th tr (middle of fan) from previous row, ch 8 join to last tr with a sl st, sl st up the last 3 stitches to get to the beginning of the next row.

**Row 3:** Ch 3, tr 5 into 4th ch from hook to form a fan, join with a sl st to the 3rd ch along from the bottom st of the fan to finish the fan, ch 5, join with a sl st to the 6th ch along from the last join, tr 6 into 3rd st along from last join to form one more fan.

**Row 4:** Ch 8, join with a sl st to 4th tr (middle st of fan) from previous row, ch 5 and join with a sl st to 6th st along from previous row, ch 6 and join with a sl st to 6th st along (middle of fan), ch 8 and join with a sl st to last st of the fan from previous row, sl st up last 3 stitches.

Row 3 and row 4 form the pattern, increasing by either a loop or a fan with each row. Repeat these 2 rows until you can count 28 fans up along the diagonal side of the shawl ending with row 3 (you can increase by an extra 4 rows if you want to make it bigger).

**Final row:** This row finishes the lace pattern. Ch 6, join with a sl st to 4th tr (middle st of fan) from previous row *Ch 3 and join with a sl st to 6th st along from previous row, ch 3 and join with a sl st to 4th tr (middle of fan from previous row)*.
Repeat from * to * until you reach the middle st of the last fan at the end of the row, ch 6 and join with a sl st to the end st in the fan.

## Ruffle-edge pattern

Start working from where you ended the last row. Ch 3 (work 3 tr into the big space created by the last stitch of the fan below, work 3 tr into the next big space in between the fans). Repeat inside the brackets to the end of the row. Tr 6 into the bottom stitch of the fan to turn the corner then repeat inside the brackets for the second side. At the end of this row you need to work tr 12 into the big space to turn the corner again.

Continue across the top of the shawl working 3 tr into each space until you reach the other corner, tr 11 into the big space. Link to the first st with a sl to finish the row. Ch 3, tr 2 into every st all the way round the outside of the shawl, except at the corners where you tr 6, until you get to the first stitch and link with a sl to finish the row.

**To finish:** Fasten off and weave in the ends.

# Marshmallow

*Angora has a fuzzy, halo effect to soften your look*

## Tension

12 treble sts over 4in (10cm)

## Materials

• 1 x 50g ball Angel yarns 100% Angora DK or other similar DK yarn
• 5mm crochet hook

*Abbreviations are on page 123*

## Pattern

**Row 1:** Ch 3 and tr 2 into first ch to form a fan of 3 stitches, turn.

**Row 2:** Ch 3, tr 2 into same space to form another fan, ch 1, tr 3 into the last st to form 2nd fan, turn.

**Row 3:** Ch 3, tr 2 into first st, ch 1, tr 3 into ch space between 2 fans, tr 3 into end stitch again, turn.

**Row 4 and all other rows:** Continue working as for row 3, increasing 1 fan at each end of the row and creating little fans in the ch sp between the fans from the previous rows. Keep going like this until you reach the end of the ball and fasten off at the end of the row.

**To finish:** Weave in ends. Agitate the angora by rubbing the fabric together to make it fluffy and soft.

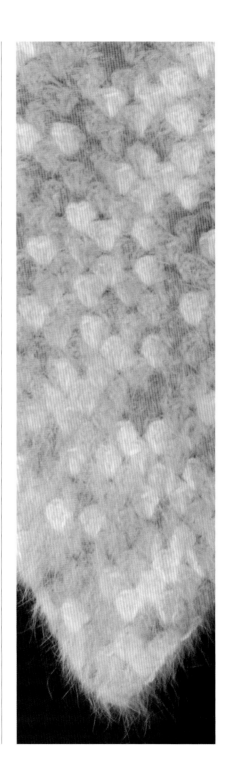

# Primrose

*The perfect little shawl to
throw over an evening dress*

## Tension

12 treble sts over 4in (10cm)

## Materials

• 2 x 50g balls Rowan Kidsilk Haze, or
other similar lace-weight yarn
• 4.5mm crochet hook

*Abbreviations are on page 123*

## Pattern

**Row 1:** Ch 4, tr 2 into first ch sp to
form a little fan, turn.

**Row 2:** Ch 3, tr 2 into first st, ch 1, tr 3
into last st, turn.

**Row 3:** Ch 3, tr 2 into first st, ch 1, tr 3
into ch sp between the next 2 fans,
ch 1, tr 3 into last st, turn.

**Row 4:** Ch 3, tr 2 into first st, *ch 1, tr 3
into ch sp between the next 2 fans*,
repeat from * to * until the end of
the row, tr 3 into last st.

**Rows 5–51:** Repeat row 4, increasing
by 1 fan at each end to create a big
triangle.

## Scalloped edge

You will now work the scalloped
edge round the outside of the shawl.
Ch 4 and link with a sl st into the
space between the fan you have just
worked and the fan below. Continue
to ch 4 and sl st into the spaces in
between the fans all the way round
the edge of the shawl until you
reach the starting fan.

Ch 4 into the very first ch st (the tip
of the triangle), then ch 4 into all the
other spaces all along the second
edge. When you reach the next
corner, work the sl st into the last st
(the tip of the triangle).

Continue to ch 4 and sl st into the
spaces until you reach the start of
this row.

To make the scallops, you will work a
series of double and treble stitches
into each 4 ch loop made in the
previous row. Sl st into the first ch
link to start. Dc 1, tr 6, dc1 into each
ch loop all the way round the
outside of the shawl.

**To finish:** When you get back to the
start, link to the first scallop with
a sl st and fasten off. Tie in ends.

# Shrugs

*These garments are simple to work up, as most of them are wide scarves.*

*Some can be joined at each end to form sleeves.*

# Jasmine

*This shrug looks great with jeans for a casual look*

## Tension

12 treble sts over 4in (10cm)

## Materials

• 4 x 50g balls Debbie Bliss Cashmerino SuperChunky or similar chunky yarn
• 8mm crochet hook

*Abbreviations are on page 123*

## Pattern

**First sleeve Row 1:** Ch 61, join with a sl st to form a circle.

**Row 2:** Ch 5 and tr 1 into first chain stitch to form a little circle.
*(Ch 1 and tr 1 into 2nd st along) repeat 3 more times.
Tr 1 into 4th st along.
(Ch 1 and tr 1 into 2nd st along) repeat 3 more times*.
Ch 3 and tr 1 into same st to form another little circle.

Repeat from * to * until you reach the first circle you made in this row. You will need to miss out 1 set of tr 1 and ch 1 as you are joining to the first st so make sure at this point you have the same amount of trebles on each side and link to the 2nd ch st in the first circle to complete the row. You should have 5 rows of trebles running in between each little circle.

**Row 3:** Sl st across the top of the next 2 stitches. Ch 5 and tr 1 into same st to form a little circle.
+(Tr 1 into every st) 8 more times.
Tr 1 into 5th st along and (tr 1 into every st) 8 more times+.
Ch 3 and tr 1 into same st to form a circle.
Repeat from + to + until you reach the end of the row. You will need to

miss out 1 tr in this side as you are joining to the first st so check that you have the same amount of trebles on each side and link to the 2nd chain on the first stitch to complete the row. Sl st 2 sts along the top of the next 2 sts to get to the middle of the first circle.

Repeat rows 2 and 3 until you have the right length for your arm – try it on occasionally to check. The length for this one was 8 sets of rows 2 and 3 together. When the length is right you will start to work on the back so you do not need to sl st 2 across the top for this last row.

## Back

You will now work on the back section. This is worked in a flat piece so you will be working to and fro.

Ch 3 to form the first st.
*(Ch 1 and tr 1 into 2nd st along) repeat 3 more times.
Tr 1 into 4th st along.
(Ch 1 and tr 1 into 2nd st along) repeat 3 more times*.
Ch 3 and tr 1 into same st to form another little circle.
Repeat in pattern until you reach the end of the row, you should have 5 sets of trebles on each side of the back opening. Turn.

Ch 3 (the next st you will work into the same st again).

+(Tr 1 into every st) 8 more times.

Tr 1 into 5th st along and (tr 1 into every st) 8 more times+.

Ch 3 and tr 1 into same st to form a circle.

Repeat in pattern until you reach the end of the row, you should have 9 sets of trebles on each side of the back opening for this row. Turn.

Work these 2 rows until you have a wide enough section for your back, try it on periodically until you have the right fit. This one was 12 sets of both rows.

On the last row ch 3 then link to the other edge of the same row to form a circle again. Turn to work the other way round.

## Second sleeve

You will now carry on working in the round for the second sleeve. Sl st 2 along top of the 3 ch you made from the last row joining the 2 edges together so you are in the middle of the 3.

Repeat rows 2 and 3 from the first sleeve until you have the same amount of rows as the first arm ending with an extra row of row 2 so it's the same on both sides.

**To finish:** Bind off and tie in ends.

# Foxglove

*A sophisticated shrug
to keep you warm on chilly days*

## Tension

18 treble sts over 4in (10cm)

## Materials

• 5 x 50g hanks Artesano Alpaca or other similar DK yarn (variegated colourway shown)
• 5mm crochet hook

*Abbreviations are on page 123*

## Pattern

**Row 1:** Ch 4, tr 2 into first ch, turn.

**Row 2:** Ch 3, tr 2 into first st, tr 3 into next st, turn.

**Rows 3–8:** Ch 3, tr 2 into first st, tr 1 into all other st till you reach the end of the row, tr 3 into last st.

**Rows 9–20:** You will now start decreasing by 1 st at the beginning of the row, working a single tr into all other sts until the end of the row. Ch 3, work a decrease st in the first 2 sts, tr 1 into every st until you reach the end of the row, turn (you should end up with 12 tr sts at the end of row 20).

**Row 21:** Ch 3, tr 4 into first st, (tr 1 into 3rd st along, tr 5 into 3rd st along) repeat to the end of the row, working 5 tr into last st.

**Rows 22–27:** Ch 3, tr 4 into first st, *tr 1 into 2nd st along (middle st of fan below), tr 5 into 3rd st along (on top of single tr st below)*. Repeat from * to * to the end of the row making sure you tr 5 into the last st again.

**Row 28:** Ch 3, tr 2 into first st, *tr 1 into 2nd st along (above middle st of fan below), tr 5 into 3rd st along (over single tr st below)*. Repeat from * to * to the end of the row, tr 3 into last st.

**Row 29:** Ch 3, *tr 5 into 3rd st along (above single tr st below) tr 1 into 3rd st along (above single tr st below)*. Repeat from * to * until the last st, tr 1.

**Row 30:** Ch 3, tr 2 into first st (above single tr st below), *tr 1 into 3rd st along (above middle st of fan below), tr 5 into 3rd st along (above single tr below)*. Repeat to the end of the row, tr 3 into last st. Repeat these 2 rows until the shawl is long enough. Measure it round your body so it will wrap comfortably and tie in front of your chest.

End with row 29 before you start to decrease. Ch 3, tr 1 into 3rd st along (above middle st of fan below) tr 5 into 3rd st along, continue in pattern until the end of the row. Repeat this decrease row 6 times (or until you match the other side if you have made any adjustments). Ch 3, tr 1 into every st to the end of the row (22 sts). Ch 3, decrease by working 2 tr sts below together (see page 120) until the end of the row. You should have 12 sts. Increase 1 tr st at the end of every row until you reach 24 sts in the row. Tr 3 tog in a decrease st (see page 121) at the beginning and end of every row until you have 1 st left. Bind off and weave the ends in.

# Pearl

*Create a summery look
with this lovely floral shrug*

## Tension

One flower should measure 1 ½ in (4cm) from tip to tip

## Materials

• 4 x 50g balls Artesano Alpaca or similar DK yarn
• 5mm crochet hook

*Abbreviations are on page 123*

## Note

This shrug should fit up to a size 14. The pattern can easily be adapted for bigger sizes by adding extra rows of flowers.

## Pattern

**Row 1:** Ch 7, *sl st into the 4th ch from hook, ch 3 into ring just created and work a base flower unit by (tr 2, ch 3, sl st back onto the ring, ch 3, tr 2), ch 10 * Repeat from * to * for 19 flowers, then keep the same side facing and turn to work the other side of the petals to complete.

**Row 2 :** *Ch 3, sl st into ring at the centre of the flower, ch 3 (tr 2, ch 3, sl st) into ring, ch 3, tr 2 and sl st into 3rd st along the base chain which connects the flowers, ch 7 (to form a loop) and sl st to the 3rd st along the base chain again (this should be where the petal starts for the next flower) * repeat from * to * into next and each flower to the end, turn. Check that each base flower is not twisted before you work into it.

**Row 3:** Ch 11, sl st into 4th ch from hook, ch 3, tr 2 into ring, ch 3, sl st into top of ch 3 of centre petal of first flower you made in the previous row, * ch 10, sl st into 4th ch from hook, ch 3, tr 2, sl st into 4th st of 7ch loop from previous row, ch 3 (sl st into ring, ch 3, tr 2) into same ring, tr 2, ch 3, sl st into top of 3rd ch of centre petal of next flower in the previous row; repeat from * to the end, turn.

**Row 4:** Ch 9, miss 2 ch stitches, sl st into next ch, * ch 3, sl st into ring, ch 3, work (tr 2, ch 3, sl st into ring, ch 3, tr 2) into same ring, miss 2 ch sts, sl st into next ch, ch 7, miss (ch 3, sl st and next ch 2) sl st into next ch st; repeat from * ending with ch 3, sl st into ch ring at the centre of the last flower, ch 3, tr 2 into ring and turn.

**Row 5:** * Ch 10, sl st into 4th ch from hook, ch 3, tr 2 into ring, sl st into 4th ch of next loop from previous row, ch 3 (sl st, ch 3, tr 2) into same ring as last 2 tr stitches * * ch 3, sl st into top of 3rd ch of centre petal of next flower from previous row; repeat from * ending last repeat at * *, turn.

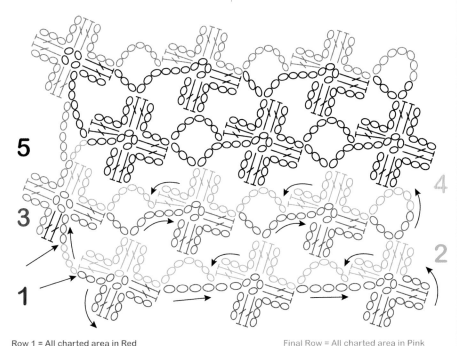

Row 1 = All charted area in Red
Row 2 = All charted area in Green
Row 3 = All charted area in Blue
Row 4 = All charted area in Orange

Final Row = All charted area in Pink

Repeat 2nd, 3rd, 4th and 5th rows 6 times. However, if you wish to make the sleeves wider you will need to add an extra set of rows.

## Joining the sleeves

You will now start the last set of flowers from rows 2–4 but on the 5th row you will need to join the sleeves together to complete the flower pattern and create a sleeve – check how the flowers are joined on previous rows and link up the same stitches to form a tube for the sleeve. Join for 6 flowers and then work on one side only to produce the back of the shrug. Work 7 sets of flowers for the back and then join both sides again making sure to line up the flowers properly to the end of the second sleeve, following how the flowers are linked up as in previous rows.

Complete edge flowers on the last sleeve: *3ch, [sl st, 3ch, 2tr, 3ch, sl st, 3ch, 2tr] all into ch ring at centre of edge flower, miss 3ch, sl st into next ch * *, 6ch, sl st into last ch before centre petal of next edge flower; rep from * ending last rep at * * after last edge flower.

**To finish:** Tie in ends. Press lightly with a cool iron on wool setting with a damp dishcloth over the shrug to flatten the flowers slightly. Be careful – ironing without a damp cloth could damage the fabric.

# Daisy

*This little cardigan is fun to make and looks stunning on*

## Tension

12 treble sts over 4in (10cm)

## Materials

• 5 x 50g balls Rowan Kidsilk Haze or similar lace-weight yarn
• 5mm crochet hook
• 40in (100cm) ribbon

*Abbreviations are on page 123*

## Note

The cardigan should fit up to a size 14. It is easy to adapt to bigger or smaller sizes by adding or taking away rows at the beginning.

## Pattern

**Row 1:** Ch 60, join with a sl st to form a circle.

**Row 2:** Ch 3, tr 2 into the same st so you will have a fan of 3 stitches coming from the same st. Tr 3 into the 3rd st along until you reach the end of the row. Join with a sl st to the first st at the top to complete this row.

**Rows 3–14:** Repeat row 2, working the fans into the space between the fans in the last row to form a lattice pattern.

**Row 15:** Ch 2 and tr 1 into every st until you reach the end, join to the first st to finish the row (this row will have the ribbon woven through at the end).

**Rows 16–30:** You can measure the arms at this point to make more or fewer rows to fit. Repeat row 2, continuing to work the fans into the spaces between the fans of the previous row. You will now open up the round to work on the back section. This part is then worked back and forth.

**Row 31:** Ch 2 and tr 2 into the same st as for row 2 to create the fan of 3 sts.

Tr 3 into the 3rd st along again carrying on in the pattern until you reach the last fan. Work 1 tr into the last st and turn.

**Rows 32–60:** For a true custom fit, hold it up against your back from time to time to see if you want it bigger or smaller.

Repeat row 31. Close to form the second sleeve when the back is at the desired length, making sure you have the same number of fans in the second sleeve as you did in the first. Repeat row 2 and work for 14 rows. Repeat row 15. Repeat row 2 and work 15 rows.

## Lacy cuffs

Work this on both ends of the sleeves to form pretty ruffles. Ch 2 and tr 1 into same st. Tr 2 into every st until you reach the end, join with a sl st to finish the row. Repeat this row once more and fasten off, tie in ends. Sl st to the inside edge of one of the arms and ch 2, work a row of tr 1 all the way round the outside of the back evenly spaced so you get a border going all the way round, join with a sl st to the first st to complete the row.

## Front

You will now work 2 triangles to form the front of your cardigan. Ch 3 and tr 2 into the first st to form a fan of 3 stitches, turn. Ch 3 and tr 2 into the first st, tr 3 into the last st, turn. Ch 3 and tr 2 into the first st, tr 3 into the 3rd st along (this should be the space between the fans from the previous row), tr 3 into the last st, turn. Carry on like this until you have a triangle of 14 rows, fasten off. You will now join these triangles centrally under the armpit section. Sl st to the end of the triangle and chain a length to form the tie, you can vary this from 12–18in (30–45cm). Joining with a sl st at the edge where the back meets one of the ends of the triangles, work a row of tr 1 evenly spaced round the outside edge of the triangle and down both sides of the chained tie section so you end up with a row of trebles all the way round the outside of the cardigan.

## Lacy edging

Starting at the edge of one of the triangles ch 3 and tr 2 into the same st, tr 2 into every st all the way round the 2 sides of the back, the ends of the triangles and down the chains for the ties so you are making a ruffle round every edge possible, join with a sl st to the first st to finish the row. Work another row the same way by ch 3 and working 2 tr into every stitch all the way round again. Fasten off and tie in ends.

**To finish:** Cut the length of ribbon in half. Weave each piece through the row of single trebles in the arms.

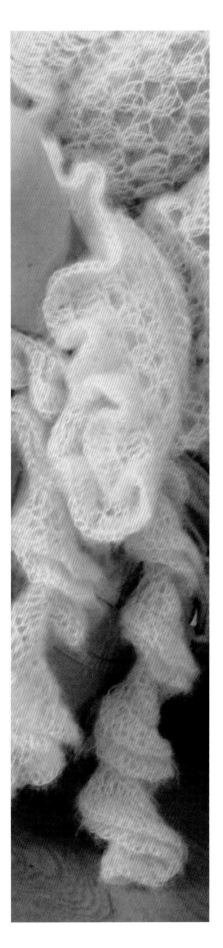

# Capelets

*Fast and fun projects, capelets are ideal garments to try after you have mastered some basic stitches.*

# Holly

*Add a glamorous touch with this sparkly little cape*

## Tension

7 treble sts over 4in (10cm)

## Materials

- 11 x 25g balls Adriafil Decor
- 10mm crochet hook

*Abbreviations are on page 123*

## Pattern

**Row 1:** Ch 40, turn.

**Row 2:** Ch 3, tr 1 into first st,*tr 1 into next st, tr 2 into following st* repeat from * to * to the end making sure you work 2 tr into the last st as per knitting note, turn.

**Row 3:** Ch 3, tr 1 into first st, tr 1 into every stitch until you reach the end. Tr 2 into the last stitch, turn.

**Row 4:** Repeat row 3.

**Row 5:** Repeat row 2.

**Row 6:** Repeat row 3.

**Row 7:** Repeat row 3.

**Row 8:** Repeat row 3.

**Row 9:** Repeat row 2.

**Row 10:** Repeat row 3.

**Row 11:** Repeat row 3.

**Row 12:** Repeat row 3.

**To finish:** Fasten off, weave in ends

## Note

You will always work 2 stitches into the first and last stitch of every row until you reach the end of the cape. This helps to increase the stitches and forms the asymmetrical drape at the front.

# Bluebell

*Made in cotton, this is ideal for a summer's evening*

## Tension

6 chain sts over 4in (10cm)

## Materials

• 3 x 50g balls Rowan Cotton Braid or similar cotton yarn
• 10mm crochet hook

*Abbreviations are on page 123*

## Pattern

**Row 1:** Ch 60. Join the ends to form a circle. This is the neckline.

**Row 2:** Ch 4 and link to 3rd chain along. Repeat until you reach the end of the circle. You should have 20 little loops.

**Rows 3–11:** Sl st into one of the loops until you reach the middle of the loop. Ch 4 stitches and link to the next loop along. Repeat until you reach the end of the circle.

**Rows 12–16:** Sl st 1 up the loop, ch 2, tr 6 to form the first shell. Tr 6 into the next loop and continue round until you reach the end of the row, then link to the last treble to form a circle again.

**To finish:** Fasten off after the last row and weave in the ends.

# Snowdrop

*Snuggle up in the winter in this super-soft capelet*

## Tension

15 treble sts over 4in (10 cm)

## Materials

• 2 x 50g balls Angel yarns 100% Angora or similar fluffy DK yarn
• 5mm crochet hook

*Abbreviations are on page 123*

## Pattern

**Row 1:** Ch 106, join with a sl st to form a circle.

**Row 2:** Ch 3, tr 1 into every st until you reach the end of the row, join with a sl st to complete the row.

**Row 3–4:** Repeat row 2. You will now split open the work and crochet back and forth increasing 1 st on the ends on both sides of each row to create the asymmetrical shape.

**Row 5:** Ch 3, tr 1 into the same st. Tr 1 into every st until you reach the last st where you will tr 2 into the same st.

**Row 6–26:** Repeat row 5.

## Scalloped edge

Create the scallops by working 6 tr into each evenly sp st. Start by working the scallops up on the inside split, working up towards the neckline area. Ch 1, tr 6 into the top end of the first st of row 25, sl st to the top end of the first st of row 24. Tr 6 into the top end of the first st of row 23, sl st into the top end of the first st of row 22. Carry on working like this until you reach the bottom edge of the other side of the split.

You should have 11 scallops down each side so 22 altogether so far. Work the scallops along the bottom edge of the capelet again by doing the same st, this time you will work it into every 4 tr stitches along and sl st the edges into the stitches in between. Ch 1, tr 6 into the 2nd st along on the bottom edge of the capelet. Sl st into the 2nd st along to finish the fan. Carry on like this until you reach the end of the row and fasten off and weave the ends in.

# Flower

Ch 4 and join with a sl st to form a circle. Ch 3 and tr 11 stitches into the centre. Ch 4 and join with a sl st to the 2nd st along, do this 5 more times to form 6 little loops. Sl st to the bottom of the first st to finish the row. Ch 1 and dc 1 into the first loop. Tr 6 into the same loop then dc 1 to finish the first petal. Work the other 5 petals the same way.

You will now form an inside layer of petals. Do this by creating an extra set of loops in the same places where you made the first set of petals. You will layer this set of loops on top of the ones you made before so they will stick up in front of the last petals. Ch 3 and join with a sl st to the 2nd tr stitch coming from the centre of the circle – this should already have a petal starting from it. Ch 3 and join with a sl st to the 2nd one along again until you have formed a circle of little loops again. Repeat until you have gone all the way round. Ch 1, dc 1, tr 4, dc 1 into first loop to form the first petal. Dc 1, tr 4, dc 1 into next and other loops to form the rest of the petals. Fasten off, leaving a long tail.

**To finish:** Use the long tail to sew the flower onto the space above the split in the capelet. Agitate the yarn by rubbing it all over to make it fluffy.

# Ponchos

*Simple to make and easy to wear,
these garments can be adapted to
different sizes and lengths
to suit everyone.*

# Mistletoe

*Soft and cosy, this poncho will
keep you warm on cold nights*

## Tension

7 chain sts over 4in (10cm)

## Materials

• 8 x 100g balls of Rowan Big Wool or
similar chunky yarn
• 15mm crochet hook

*Abbreviations are on page 123*

## Pattern

**Row 1:** Ch 40, join with a sl st to form
a circle.

**Row 2:** Ch 3, tr 3 into first st to form
a fan of 4 st. This will be the front of
the poncho. Tr 19 (halfway round the
cirlce), tr 4 into the next st, this will
be the back of the poncho. Tr 19, join
with a sl st to the first st to complete
the row.

**Row 3:** Sl st along the top of the
stitches until you reach the middle
of the fan. Ch 3, tr 3 into the same
space in the middle of the fan.
Tr 1 into every st until you reach the
other fan, tr 4 into the middle of the
fan, tr 1 into every st until you reach
the beginning. Join with a sl st to
finish the row.

**Rows 4–17:** Repeat row 3.

**To finish:** Cut 12in (30cm) lengths
from the rest of the yarn to make
the tassels. I used two strands to
make each tassel. Fold the strands in
half. Thread the looped end into one
of the spaces between the yarn on
the last row. Feed the ends through
and secure.

# Rose

*This versatile poncho is just a
long scarf, joined at one end*

## Tension

13 treble sts over 4in (10cm)

## Materials

• 5 x 50g balls Sirdar Sublime Kid
Mohair or similar DK yarn
• 2 x 100g balls Rowan Biggy Print or
other chunky variegated slub yarn
• 6mm crochet hook

*Abbreviations are on page 123*

## Note

Make the main piece up with the Kid
Mohair and use the Biggy Print to
weave through and form the tassels.

## Pattern

**Row 1:** Using the Kid Mohair yarn, ch
150, turn. Ch 2, dc 1 into every st to
the end of the row, turn.

**Rows 2–3:** Ch 2, dc 1 into every st to
the end of the row, turn.

**Row 4:** Ch 3, tr 1 into every st to the
end of the row

**Rows 5–14:.** Repeat rows 1–4 10 more
times. Do 3 more rows of single
crochet and bind off.

You will now have one long scarf.

**To make up:** Join the two ends of the
scarf together and decide how big
you want your neckline to be. I left
about 16–17in (40–43cm) at the
folded end of the scarf. Slip stitch
the top side together leaving the
neckline opening at the fold of the
scarf. Tie a little knot at the end of
the Biggy Print yarn and weave it
through the holes in the poncho,
weaving from one side to the other.
Pull it through the other side, leaving
about 4–6in (10–15cm) on both ends.
Cut the yarn and repeat until you
have finished weaving through all
the holes.

**To finish:** Cut the remaining Biggy
Print yarn into 10in (25cm) tassels.
Thread them one at a time into the
last hole on the poncho where the
other yarn pokes out and secure into
a knot neatly at the end of the
poncho. The tassel will now be made
up of three strands of yarn. Trim to
desired length.

# Lily

*A lovely, light poncho
to wear on spring days*

## Tension

9 chain sts over 4in (10cm)

## Materials

• 4 x 25g balls Sirdar Sublime Kid
Mohair or similar DK yarn
• 10mm crochet hook

*Abbreviations are on page 123*

## Pattern

**Row 1:** Ch 66 st. Join to form a circle with a sl st. This forms the neckline. You will work in one direction in the round from now on until you finish.

**Row 2:** Ch 2, tr 5 into same st to form a fan of 6 st. *Tr 3 into 3rd chain link * and repeat until halfway round the neckline (you should have 10 little fans and 1 bigger fan). Tr 6 into the next 3rd chain link and repeat from * to * until you reach the first big fan. Join this with a sl st to form row 2.

**Row 3:** Sl st 3 across the top of the next 3 st until you reach the middle of the fan (you should have 3 tr st on either side). Ch 2, tr 5 into the same stitch to form the bigger fan again (6 st). * * Tr 3 into the space between the big fan and next fan on first row. Repeat treble stitches 3 times into the spaces between the fans until you reach the other big fan * *. Tr 6 into the middle of this to make the big fan again. Repeat from * * to * * until you get to the end of the row and sl st to the first big fan again to make row 3.

**Rows 4–17:** Repeat row 3.

**To finish:** To make the tassels, cut the remaining yarn into 12in (30cm) lengths. Fold three lengths in half for each tassel and thread the looped end into the space between two fans. Thread the ends through the loop and pull them through.

# Marigold

*This is also great as a summer cover-up on the beach*

## Tension

6 chain sts over 4in (10cm)

## Materials

• 5 x 50g balls Rowan Cotton Braid or similar cotton ribbon yarn
• 10mm crochet hook

*Abbreviations are on page 123*

## Materials

You will work 1 strand of each colour together at all times. Work the semi-circle first, then work the rest of the shawl round it.

## Pattern

**Row 1:** Ch 60. Join the ends to form a circle. This is your neckline.

**Row 2:** *Ch 6 and sl st into the same stitch to form a little loop. This will be the front (or back) of the poncho. Ch 4 and sl st it to the 3rd link along on the neckline. Keep doing this until you reach halfway along the neckline*. You should have 2 big loops and about 10 little loops in between.
Repeat from * to * to form the 2nd half of the first row.

Make sure the circle and loops are flat and they don't get twisted up when you start the third row.

**Row 3:** Sl st 3 up the first loop to end up one third of the way round the loop.
*Ch 6 and link to the other side of the loop about one third of the way round. You should now have one loop on top of another. Ch 4 and join with a sl st to the next small loop. Keep doing this until you reach the other big loop. Ch 4 to join with a sl st to the big loop about one third of the way up*.
Repeat from * to * for the 2nd side of the row.

**Rows 4–20:** Repeat the 3rd row. Fasten off at the end of the last row and weave in the ends

**To finish:** Cut three 10–12in (25–30cm) lengths of yarn and thread through the loops to form the tassels.

# Hats & Mittens

*A selection of accessories for wintery days, these are quick and easy to make and are great last-minute gifts as well!*

# Raspberry

*This essential raspberry beret
is bound to get you noticed*

## Tension

20 chain sts over 4in (10cm)

## Materials

• 1 x 50g ball Angel yarns 100%
angora or other similar
DK fluffy yarn
• 4mm crochet hook

*Abbreviations are on page 123*

## Note

This project is worked from the
centre of the hat out.

## Pattern

**Row 1:** Ch 4, join with a sl st to form
a circle.

**Row 2:** Ch 3, tr 11 into centre of circle,
join with a sl st to complete the row.

**Row 3:** Ch 3, tr 2 into every st all the
way round, join with a sl st to
complete the row, 24 st.

**Row 4:** Ch 3. (Tr 2 into next st, tr 1)
repeat to the end, join with a sl st to
complete the row.

**Row 5:** Ch 3. (Tr 2 into next st, tr 1 into
next 2 sts) repeat to the end, join
with a sl st to complete the row.

**Row 6:** Ch 3. (Tr 2 into next st, tr 1
into next 3 sts) repeat to the end,
join with a sl st to complete the row.

**Row 7:** Ch 3. (Tr 2 into next st, tr 1 into
next 4 sts) repeat to the end, join
with a sl st to complete the row.

**Row 8:** Ch 3. (Tr 2 into next st, tr 1
into next 5 sts) repeat to the end,
join with a sl st to complete the row.

**Row 9:** Ch 3. (Tr 2 into next st, tr 1
into next 6 sts) repeat to the end,
join with a sl st to complete the row.
Carry on working like this, increasing
1 tr st in the bracket until you reach
10 spaces between each increase.

**To decrease:** Ch 3, work a decrease st
in the next and every 10 sts, repeat
to the end and join with a sl st to
complete the row. Ch 3, work a
decrease st in the next and every 9
sts, repeat to the end and join with a
sl st to complete the row. Ch 3,
work a decrease st in the next and
every 8 sts, repeat to the end and
join with a sl st to complete the row.
Ch 3, work a decrease st in the next
and every 7 sts, repeat to the end
and join with a sl st to complete the
row. Ch 3, work a decrease st in the
next and every 6 sts, repeat to the
end and join with a sl st to complete
the row. Ch 3, work a decrease st in
the next and every 5 sts, repeat to
the end and join with a sl st to
complete the row.

## Scalloped edge

Work a row of scallops round the bottom of the beret: ch 1 (tr 6 into 3rd st along, link to next 3rd st along with a sl st), repeat to the end, fasten off and weave in ends.

## Flower corsage

Ch 4, join with a sl st to form a circle. Ch 3, tr 11 into centre, join with a sl st to complete the row. Ch 1 (tr 6 into 2nd st along, link to the 2nd st along from that with a sl st), repeat to the end. Fasten off leaving a long tail to sew the flower onto the beret.

## Curliques

Ch 20, turn, ch 2 and dc 2 into every st until you reach the end of the row, fasten off. Ch 16, turn, ch 2 and dc 2 into every st until you reach the end of the row, fasten off. Ch 12, turn, ch 2 and dc 2 into every st until you reach the end of the row, fasten off

**To finish:** Sew the curliques onto the flower using the long tail so the curliques start from in between two petals. Sew onto the beret where you fastened off. Weave in ends.

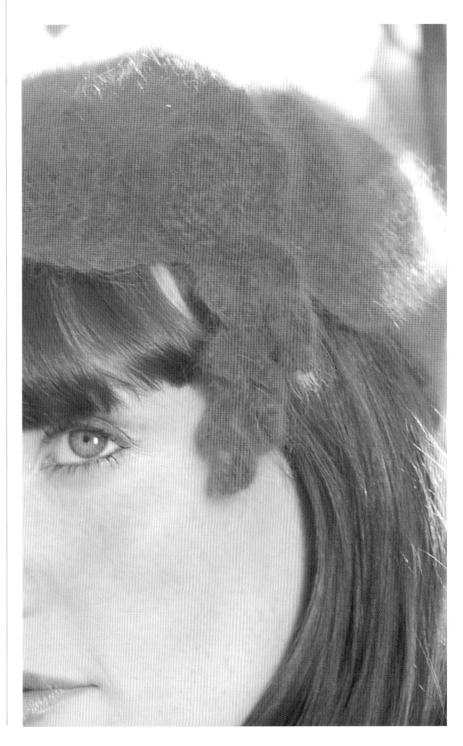

# Posy

*This simple hat, with optional flower, will keep off the chill*

## Tension

12 chain sts over 4in (10cm)

## Materials

• 1 hank Wendy Paris Mohair or any other mohair Aran-weight yarn
• 6mm crochet hook

*Abbreviations are on page 123*

## Pattern

**Row 1:** Ch 4, join with a sl st to form a circle.

**Row 2:** Ch 2, dc 7 into centre, join with a sl st to complete row.

**Row 3:** Ch 3, tr 2 into same st to form a fan of 3 sts. Tr 3 into every 2nd st along, join with a sl st to complete the row. You should have 4 fans.

*Ch 3, turn, tr 2 into sp between 2 fans below to form another fan. Tr 3 into 2nd st along, tr 3 into sp between fans below, repeat to the end, join with a sl st to complete the row*. You should now have 8 fans.

**Row 4:** Repeat row 3 from * to *. You should now have 16 fans.

**Row 5–12:** Ch 3, turn, tr 2 into sp between fans below. Tr 3 into every sp between fans again to the end of the row, join with a sl st to complete the row (you can add an extra row or two if the hat needs to be deeper).

**Row 13:** You will now work a row of scallops round the edge of the hat. Ch 3, tr 5 into sp between fans below, dc 1 round the middle post from the next fan along. Tr 6 into next sp between fans below, dc 1 round middle post from next fan along, repeat to the end of the row. Join to the first st with a sl st, fasten off and weave in ends.

## Flower (optional)

Ch 4, join with a sl st. Ch 4, sl st to
centre 5 times. You should have 5
loops. Ch 2, dc1, tr 5, dc 1 into first
loop, dc1 , tr 5, dc 1 into 2nd and all
other loops until you reach the end.
Join to the first st with a sl st. Fasten
off, leaving a long tail with which to
sew the flower onto the hat.

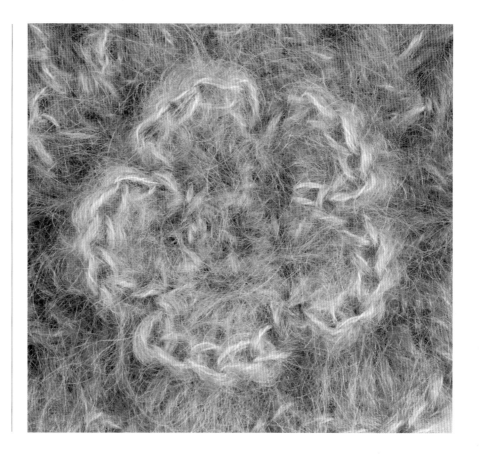

# Rainbow

*These colourful mittens are fun to make and wear*

## Tension

27 treble sts over 4in (10cm)

## Materials

- 1 hank Lucy Neatby Celestial Merino or other 4-ply yarn
- 2.5mm crochet hook
- 2 buttons to fasten cuffs

*Abbreviations are on page 123*

## Note

These mittens are worked from the wrist up to the fingers. They can be made bigger or smaller by increasing or decreasing stitches as necessary.

Just make sure you have an even amount of stitches when you start.

The cuff is worked open so you will need to turn the work when you reach the end of each row.

## Left-hand mitten

**Row 1:** Ch 50 (check now if you need to add extra stitches if your wrist is bigger, or if you need to decrease for a smaller size), turn.

**Row 2:** Ch 3 and tr 1 into every st until you reach the end of the row, turn.

**Row 3:** You will now start to work the next few rows in a rib effect stitch for the cuff. Ch 3 and wrap the yarn round the hook as for a treble stitch, then insert the hook from in front and from right to left round the stem of the treble stitch below. Grab the yarn and pull back to where you started, then work the same way to complete the stitch as a normal treble. See 1 and 2.

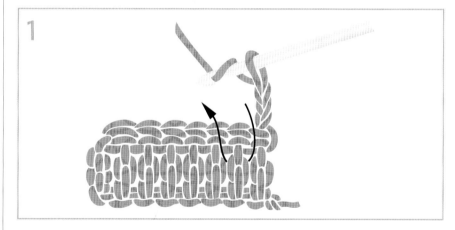

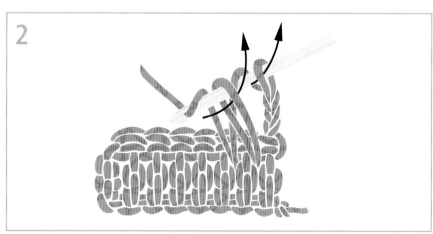

Wrap the yarn round the hook again and insert the hook from behind and from the right to the left round the stem of the treble stitch below,

grab the yarn and pull back to where you started then work the same way to complete the stitch as a normal treble. See 3 and 4.

Repeat these 2 stitches until you reach the end of the row.

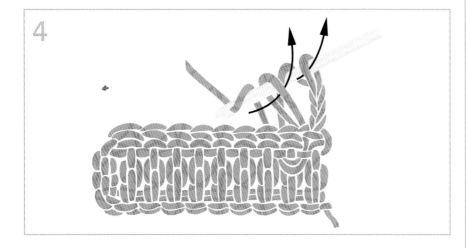

**Rows 4–7:** Work 4 further rows of ribbing, at the end of the last row join with a sl st to the beginning of the row to form a circle.

**Row 8:** This row and all other rows are worked in normal, not raised treble stitches. Ch 3, work a decrease st in the next and every 9th st along until you finish the row, 45 st.

Decrease by wrapping the yarn round the hook and inserting the hook into the next stitch. Wrap the yarn, draw the loop through, wrap the yarn and draw through 2 of the loops on hook. Leave the last loop on the hook so you have 2 loops left on the hook. Repeat this into the next stitch so you have 3 loops on the hook. Wrap the yarn and draw through all 3 loops on hook – 1 treble decreased.

**Rows 9–17:** Ch 3, tr 1 into every st and join with a sl st at the end of the row to complete the row.

**Row 18:** You will now work the hole for the thumb in the next 2 rows. Ch 3, tr 1 into every st 18 times, ch 11, miss 5 ch sp and tr 1 into 6th ch and every st until you reach the end of the row. Join with a sl st to complete the row.

**Row 19:** Ch 3, tr 1 into every st until you reach the ch loop, join with a sl st to 3rd ch along in loop, sl st 5 times across the top of the loop leaving 3 sp at the end, tr 1 into first st back on the main body of the mitten, tr 1 into every st until the end and join with a sl st to complete the row.

**Row 20:** Ch 3, tr 1 into every st, including the 5 sl st made from previous row across the top of the thumb 45 st.

**Rows 21–26:** Ch 3, tr 1 into every sl, join with a sl st to complete the row (you can add or remove a row at this point to custom fit the mitten to the right length for your fingers).

**Row 27:** You will now work a row of scallops across the top of the mitten. Tr 4 into 2nd st along to form a fan, join with a sl st to 2nd st along, repeat until you reach the end of the row (the last scallop will have 3 st at the end). Fasten off.

## Thumb

Join yarn with a sl st to the inside of the thumb hole, ch 3 and pick up 19 st evenly round the edge, 20 sts. Join with a sl st to form a circle and complete the row. Ch 3, tr 1 into every st all the way round again, join with a sl st. Ch 3, work a decrease st into next and every 4th tr along, 16 st. Work a row of scallops across the top of the thumb as you did in row 27.

Join yarn with a sl st to the ribbing, work a row of scallops across the bottom of the work as before in row 27, when you reach the end of the row you will now work a row of dc inside the split (2 dc into each tr sp) Work 16 dc, ch 6 (this is the buttonhole loop), join with a sl st to next tr sp, work 4 dc to the end of the split. Sl st to the bottom of the first fan and fasten off.

## Right-hand mitten

The right-hand mitten is worked the same as the left-hand mitten except for the thumb hole – this time you work 21 treble stitches instead of 18 before you open for the thumb. The rest is worked up exactly the same way.

**To finish:** Weave in all the ends. Sew the buttons onto each mitten.

# Bags

*Crochet bags are
so popular and surprisingly chic.
Make a selection in
different colours for every day
of the week.*

# Ginger

## *This colourful satchel can easily be made in a weekend*

## Tension

13 dc sts over 4in (10cm)

## Materials

- 3 x 100g hanks Noro Iro
- 6mm crochet hook
- 2–3 buttons (optional)

*Abbreviations are on page 123*

## Note

See the picture below for a variation of colour and trimmings.

## Pattern

**Row 1:** Ch 80 stitches, turn.

**Row 2–33:** Ch 2, dc 1 into every st to the end of the row.

## Main body of the bag

Fold the bag in 2, counting 31 stitches along one side so you will have a short half and a long half (this long half will later double over to make the flap for the top of the bag). At the 31st st you need to join your yarn to form the bag strap.

Work dc 1 along the short half of the bag until you reach the end, then ch 115 stitches to form the strap of the bag. Join with a sl st to the top end of the other short half and work 31 dc stitches.

To start the 2nd row you will need to work an extra st past the 31st stitch (so effectively you are working 32 stitches on this side).
You will pick up an extra stitch each time you get to the end of the next 5 rows to create a flattened bottom to the bag.

*Ch 1 and turn, join with a sl st to the last st worked on the previous row and dc 1 all the way to the end of the next row taking in the bag strap and the other half of the bag*. Repeat from * to * for 3 more rows.

You should now have 5 rows making up your bag strap. On the last row you will join the bag together by working the 2 sides together with dc st. Push the crochet hook through both the bag handle and side of the bag until you seal up the gap to form the finished item – you should end up with 31 stitches along this side so it mirrors the other side of the bag.

**To finish:** Turn the bag inside out. If you're using buttons, sew them onto the front of the bag. You can also sew poppers in if you want a secure fastening.

# Camille

*Add a little frou frou
with this fur-lined bag*

## Tension

7 treble sts over 4in (10cm)

## Materials

• 2 x 100g balls Rowan Big Wool or similar chunky yarn
• 1 x 50g ball Jaeger Fur or similar furry yarn
• 12mm crochet hook
• 1 pair of bamboo bag handles

*Abbreviations are on page 123*

## Pattern

**Row 1:** Using the Big Wool, ch 42 and join with a sl st to form a circle. Make sure the stitches are not twisted.

**Row 2:** Ch 1, dc 1 into every st until you reach the end of the circle, join with a sl st to finish row.

**Row 3:** Ch 3, tr 1 into every st until you reach the end of the circle, join with a sl st to finish the row.

**Row 4:** Repeat row 2.

**Row 5:** You will now start to increase the sides.
Ch 3, tr 1 into the same st so you have 2 stitches coming from the same place. Tr 1 into every st until you reach halfway round, tr 2 into the same st again, tr 1 into every st until you reach the end, join with a sl st to finish row.

**Row 6:** Repeat row 2.

**Row 7:** Repeat row 5.

**Row 8:** Repeat row 2.

**Row 9:** Repeat row 5.

**Row 10:** Repeat row 2.

**Row 11:** Repeat row 5.

**Row 12:** Repeat row 2.

**To make up:** Join the sides together to form the bottom of the bag. Find the points where you increased stitches and fold in half at these points so you have the increase running down the sides. Sl st the 2 sides together and fasten off.

**To finish:** Using the Jaeger Fur, work 1 row of dc 1 all round the top of the bag.

## Handles

Working on the inside of the bag,
place the bamboo handle centrally
on the inside of the bag and work
sl st over the handle into the st just
below the fur to secure the handles.
Work the other handle in the
same way.

## Note

For a more professional finish you
could line the bag using a piece of
matching fabric.

# Jelly Bean

*Deceptively spacious, this bag is big enough for all your goodies*

## Tension

8 dc sts over 4in (10cm)

## Materials

• 3 x 100g balls Sirdar Bigga or similar chunky yarn
• 12mm crochet hook
• 2 x D-shaped bamboo bag handles

*Abbreviations are on page 123*

## Note

The whole bag is made with dc stitches, even round the handles.

## Pattern

Starting with the base of the bag, this is worked back and forth in dc.

Ch 20, turn, ch 2 and dc back to the beginning. *Turn again and dc to the end*. Repeat * to* 6 times to form a rectangle. Dc all the way round the outside of the rectangle. Repeat the last row 5 times then begin to decrease.

Fold the bag in half lengthwise and place a st marker at the sides of the bag to mark the very end st – this will be the st to be decreased. Find the centre st in the middle of the front and back and mark these with a st marker too (you can use a different colour of wool and just tie it round the st loosely).

**Work the next row by decreasing 1 st at each of the sides where the markers are and once in the middle markers at the front and back**.

The next row is worked by decreasing only in the middle section but this time you decrease slightly differently. Count 4 st from the centre marker to the left and 4 st again to the right on both the front and the back. Work this row by dc 4 st (2 at the front and 2 at the back).

Repeat ** to ** for the next row.

The next row is worked round with no decrease.

The following row dc 1 st at each end again following up where the marker was placed.

Repeat the last 2 rows twice more.

**To make up:** Place one of the bag handles centrally onto the bag top and crochet round again but this time dc over and under the bag handle to incorporate it into the top of the bag. Do the same on the other side. Keep going until you reach the first handle again and start to dc round the top of the bag handle – 17 stitches to cover the handle completely. You may find you need a couple more st or less depending on how tight your crocheting is. Keep going until you reach the second handle and do the same.

**To finish:** When you have got to the end of the handle, join the yarn to the rest of the bag with a sl st and fasten off. Weave the ends in and straighten out the stitches on the bag handle.

# Materials & Equipment

*This section
contains useful information
on yarns and hooks.*

*There are also conversion charts,
to help you find substitute yarns.*

# Yarns

## *Weight equivalents*

The conversion chart below will simplify the different terms for weights of yarns.

This will help if you choose to substitute yarns for any of the projects.

| UK | USA |
|---|---|
| 2 ply | Lace weight |
| 3 ply | Light fingering |
| 4 ply | Fingering |
| 5 ply | Sport |
| 8 ply, DK | Sport or Light worsted |
| 10 ply, Aran | Worsted |
| 12 ply | Chunky |
| 14 ply | Bulky |

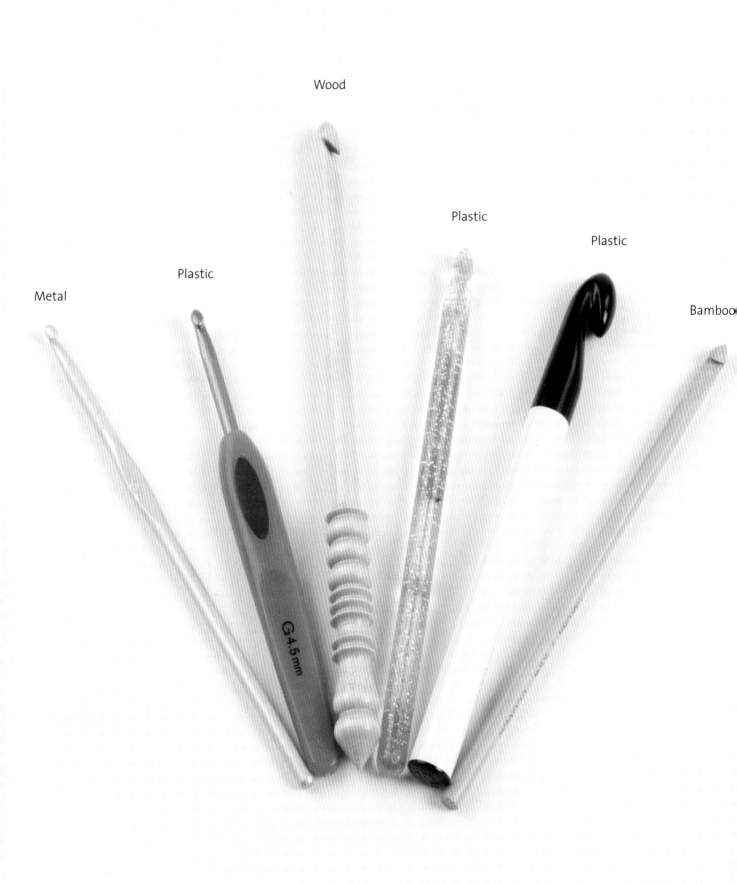

Wood

Plastic

Plastic

Metal

Plastic

Bamboo

G 4.5 mm

# Crochet hooks

There are many different types of hooks on the market. I would suggest trying a few different ones until you find the type that suits you best.

## Bamboo or wood

These are ideal for beginners as they have more friction on them, making the loop less likely to slip off the end.

## Plastic

These are also good for beginners. They are relatively cheap and come in a funky selection of colours. They are also warm to touch, so are great for people with carpal tunnel syndrome or arthritis.

## Metal

These are great all-rounders. They are fast to work with and very smooth so you can really pick up speed while working with them. Metal hooks with grips, such as the clover soft-touch ones, are also available.

## Hook sizes

The finer the yarn, the smaller the hooks size required. Experiment with different sizes and yarns to see what effects you achieve. For instance, you can use larger hooks with fine yarns to produce fast, lacy fabric.

Hook sizes, like yarns, vary between UK, US and metric terms. Use the conversion chart shown here.

| USA | Metric |
| --- | --- |
| S | 19.00mm |
| Q | 15.00mm |
| P | 12.00mm |
| O | 10.0mm |
| N | 9.00mm |
| M | 8.00mm |
| K | 7.00mm |
| – | 6.50mm |
| J | 6.00mm |
| I | 5.50mm |
| H | 5.00mm |
| G | 4.50mm |
| F | 4.00mm |
| E | 3.50mm |
| D | 3.00mm |
| C | 2.50mm |
| B | 2.00mm |
| 5 steel | 1.75mm |
| 7 steel | 1.50mm |
| 8 steel | 1.25mm |
| 10 steel | 1.00mm |

# Techniques

*This section explains
the basics of crochet using
clear instructions and
illustrations.*

*Make up crochet squares
to practise the stitches.*

# Techniques

## Holding the hook and yarn

Everyone holds their hook and yarn differently. You will find the most comfortable way for you by practising.

**1** Right-handers hold the hook in their right hand, as if it were a pencil or with a firmer grip. Your left hand holds the work and the yarn.

**2** To get the right tension for even neat work, wind the yarn round the fingers of the left hand; you will find your own way of doing this but an example is shown below.

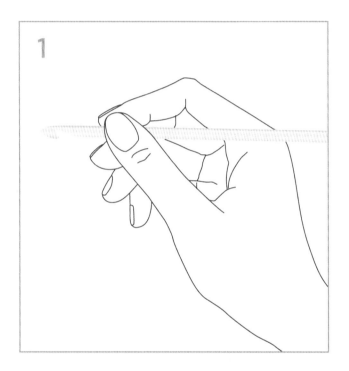

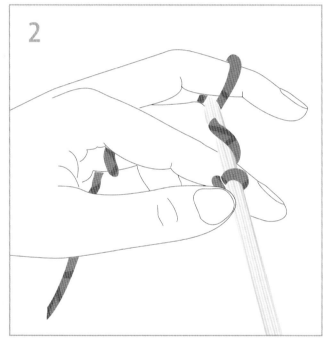

The left hand feeds the yarn and the index finger and thumb holds the work.

Left-handers, look at the images in a mirror – this will show you the correct way to hold your hook.

# The basic stitches

## *The base chain*

Most crochet begins with a base (or foundation) chain, which is a series of chain stitches.

### Chain stitch (ch)

**1** Make a slip knot. Wrap the yarn over the hook in an anticlockwise direction.

**2** Draw the yarn through to form a new loop, taking care not to tighten up the loop below.

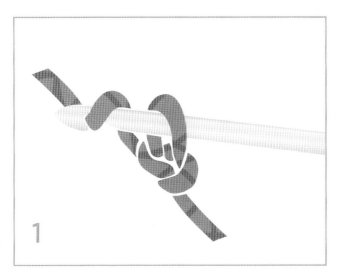

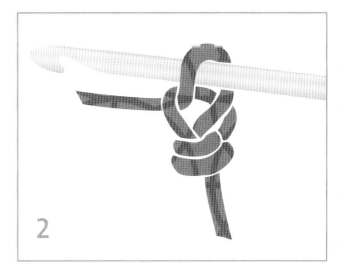

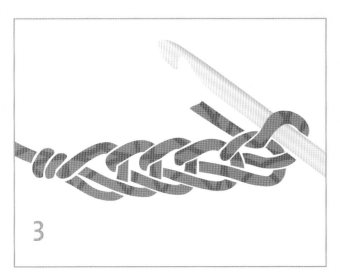

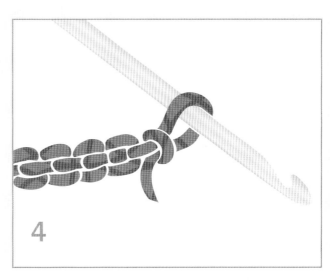

The base chain, made of five chain stitches, shown from the front.

The base chain shown from the back.

# Slip stitch (sl st)

**1** Insert the hook into 2nd chain from hook, wrap the yarn over the hook, draw the yarn through the chain and the loop on the hook in one movement.

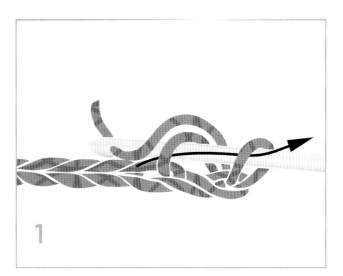

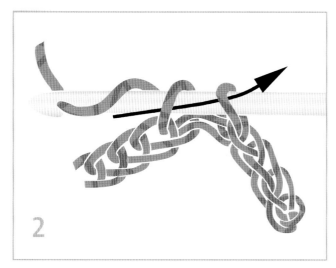

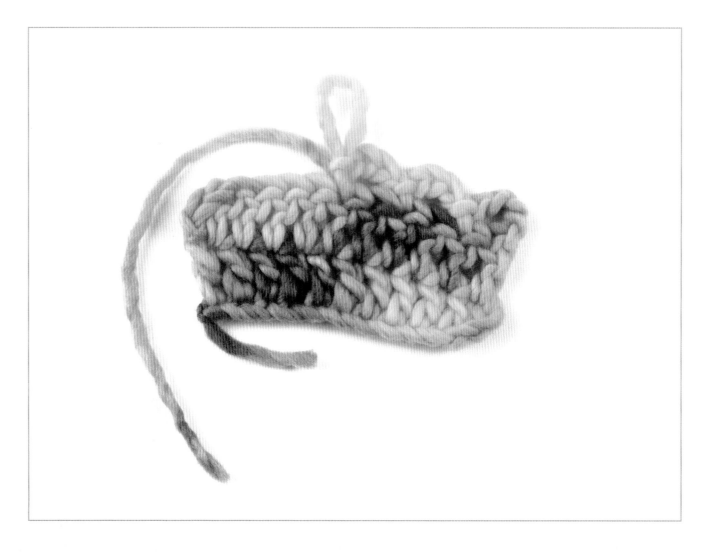

# Double crochet (dc)

**1** Insert the hook into 2nd chain from hook, wrap the yarn over the hook and draw it through the chain only.

**2** Wrap the yarn again and draw the yarn through both loops on hook.

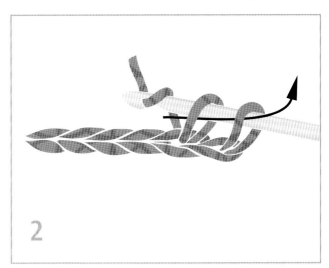

# Treble (tr)

**1** Wrap the yarn over hook and insert hook into 4th chain from hook.

**2** Wrap the yarn over the hook, draw through the chain only and wrap the yarn round again.

**3** Draw through the first 2 loops only and wrap the yarn round again.

**4** Draw through the last 2 loops on the hook.

# *Working in rows*

**1** The first row of the fabric is made by working across the base chain.

**2** Right-handers work from right to left, left-handers work from left to right. Insert hook under either one (see **1**) or two (see **2**) of the three threads that make up each individual chain. Choose which one suits you best and stick to it throughout your work to maintain stitch consistency.

At the start of the first row, some stitches are missed out to allow the fabric to stand up to its proper height. These chain stitches will stand up alongside the other stitches. This is counted as the first stitch in the row.

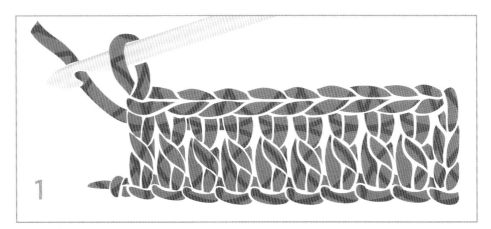

The number of chains missed depends upon the height of the stitch being used i.e. double crochet = 1 or 2 chains missed, treble = 3 chains missed. You will need to make extra chain stitches for the base chain than there are stitches required in the base row.

At the end of each row 'turn' the work so that another row can be worked across the top of the previous one again from right to left (left-handers from left to right).

It does not matter which way you turn, but whichever way you choose, stick to this to maintain neat work.

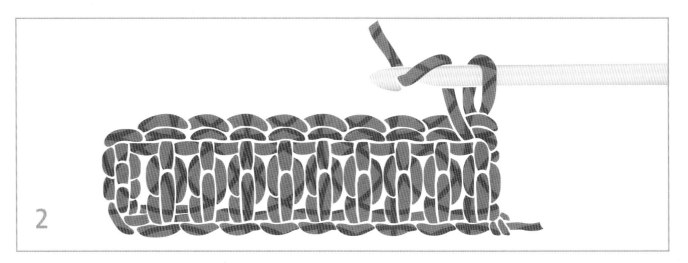

To start a new row, a turning chain (one or more single chains) must be worked to bring the hook up to the height the row will be, similar to the base row. The number of chains for turning depends upon the height of the stitch they are to match as follows: double crochet = 1 chain, treble = 3 chains.

These numbers are guidelines only. Depending on your personal technique, the type of work you are doing, the thickness of yarn and size of hook you are using, you may find, from time to time, a larger or smaller number of chains will give you better results.

The turning chain usually counts as the first stitch of the new row.

In this case miss the first stitch in the previous row.

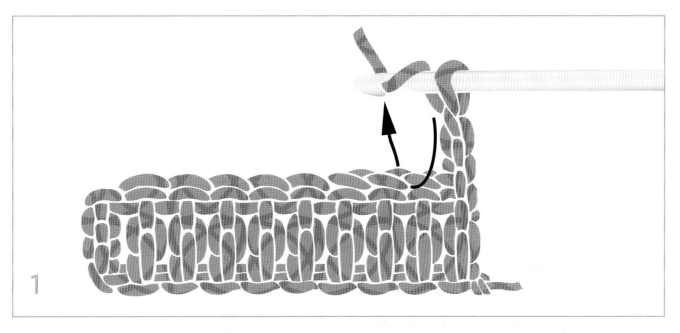

Remember to work a stitch into the top of the previous turning chain when you reach the end of the row.

To make each stitch, insert the hook under the two loops lying on top of each stitch in the previous row.

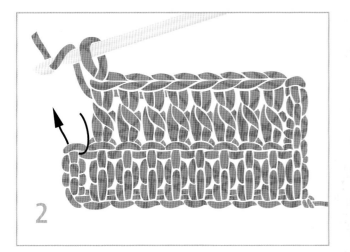

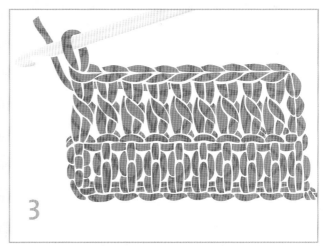

# Working in rounds

**1** To work in rounds make three or more chains, depending on the design, and join them into a ring by inserting the hook into the first of them and making a slip stitch.

**2** To begin each round make a 'starting chain' which will be the equivalent of a 'turning chain' to match the height of the stitches being used. Always insert the hook into the centre of the base chain ring when working the stitches of the first round.

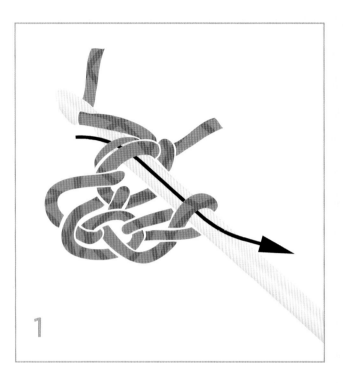

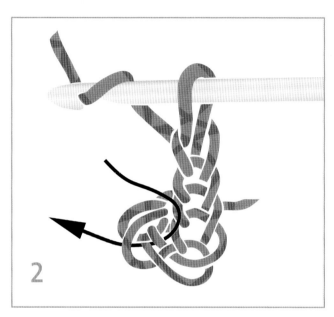

**3** From the 2nd round insert the hook under the top two loops of the stitches in the previous round.

**4** When each round is complete join the round by inserting the hook into the top of the starting chain with a slip stitch.

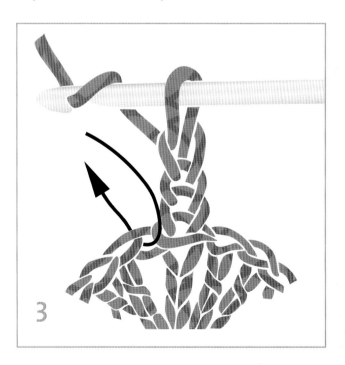

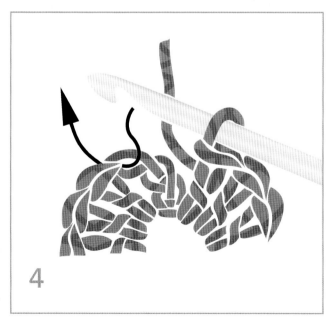

**5** Do not turn the work between rounds, but continue working with the same side facing and treat this as the 'right side' of the fabric.

**6** Fasten off with a slip stitch after joining the last stitch with the first stitch. This completes a round; do not make another chain.

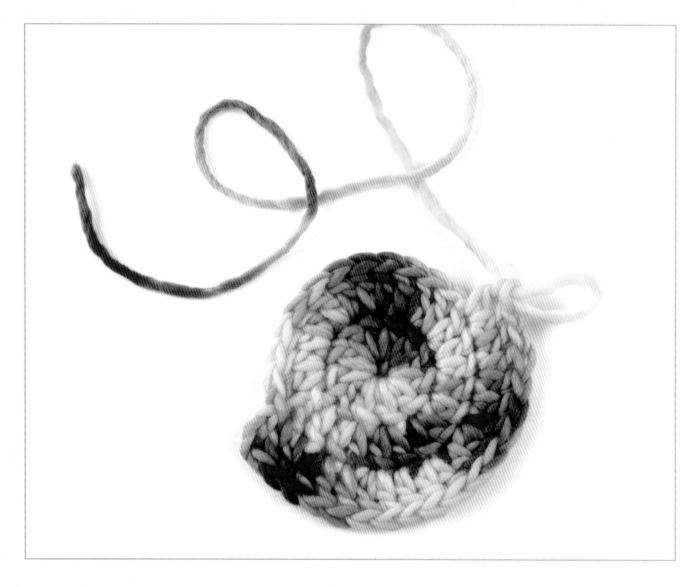

# *Increasing*

Increases are made simply by working two or more
stitches into one stitch at either or both ends of a row.

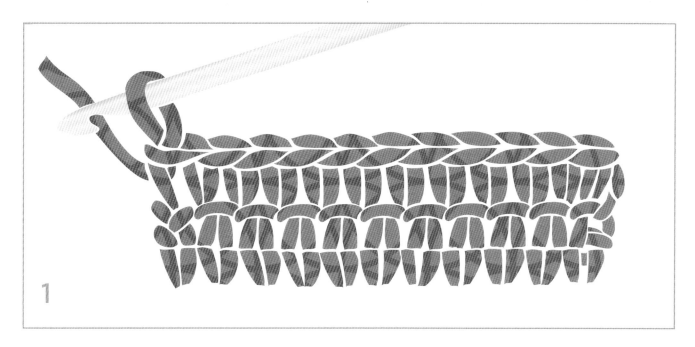

1

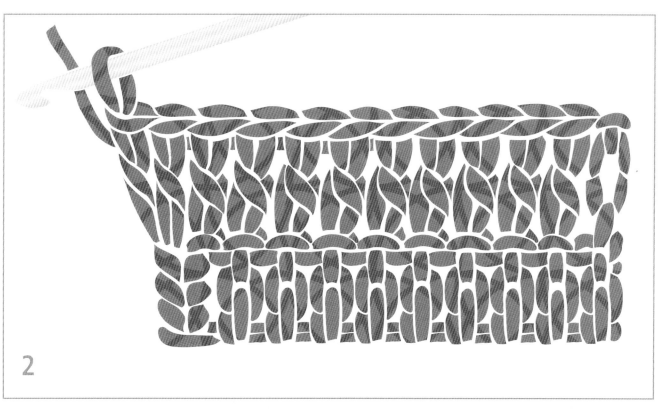

2

# Decreasing

Decreases are usually made by working two or more stitches together.

## Working two double crochet stitches together (dc2tog)

**1** Insert the hook into next stitch (or as required), wrap the yarn round the hook, and draw a loop through.

**2** Repeat this step into the next stitch (three loops on hook).

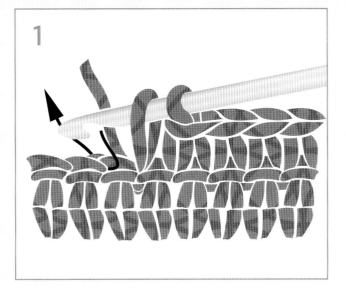

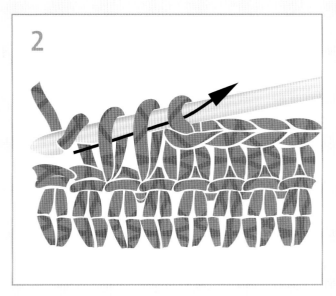

**3** Wrap the yarn and draw through all three loops on hook – one double crochet decreased.

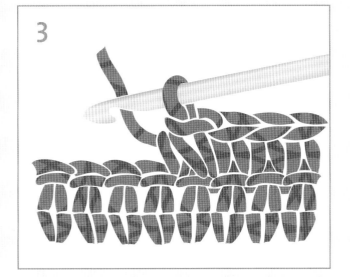

## Working three double crochet stitches together (dc3tog)

**1** Work as for dc 2 tog until there are three loops on hook. Insert hook into a third stitch, wrap the yarn and draw through a loop (four loops on the hook).

**2** Wrap the yarn and draw through all four loops on hook – two double crochet decreased.

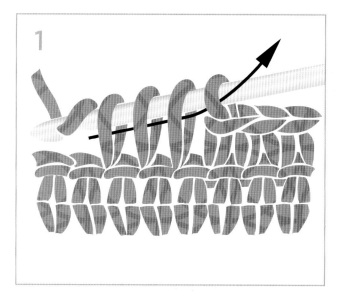

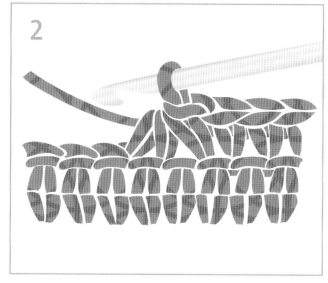

## Working two treble stitches together (tr2tog)

**1** Wrap the yarn round the hook, insert the hook into the next stitch (or as required), wrap the yarn, draw a loop through, wrap the yarn and draw through two of the loops on hook (two loops left on the hook).

**2** Repeat this step into the next stitch (three loops on the hook).

**3** Wrap the yarn and draw through all three loops on hook – one treble decreased.

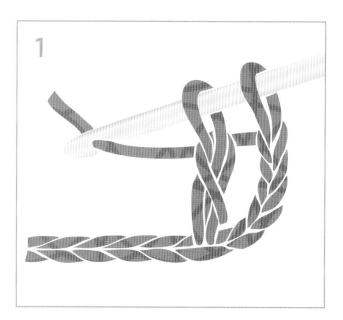

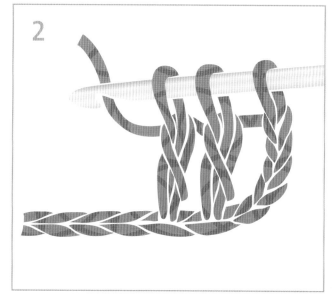

## Working three treble stitches together (tr3tog)

Work as for tr 2 tog until there are three loops on hook. Repeat step 1 once more, wrap yarn and draw through all four loops on hook – two trebles decreased.

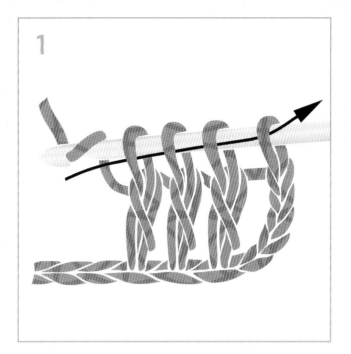

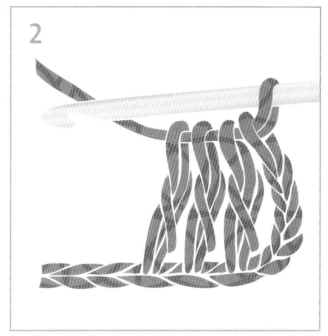

## Fastening off

To fasten off a complete piece of crochet, cut the yarn about 2in (5cm) away, draw it through the one remaining loop and tighten.

# Blocking and Finishing

## Blocking

Blocking is the process of using heat, steam or water to even out the stitches in the finished fabric which makes sewing the seams together easier and produces neater edges. It is always best to follow manufacturer's advice on the yarn label. If it is machine washable, the yarn will have a memory and machine washing will restore the original shape. Some yarns are more delicate and require a little more care.

For wet blocking, hand wash or thoroughly soak the garment and gently squeeze out as much water as possible by wrapping in a towel or putting the garment through the shortest spin in a machine. Gently pull the garment into shape and lay on a flat surface to dry. Pinning out the garment as it is drying is the best way of maintaining its shape.

To steam, use an iron or steamer about ½in (12.5mm) above the garment on the wrong side. Lay the garment flat to dry thoroughly, as it can become warped or misshapen if you don't let it completely dry out. Use pins to hold in shape if necessary.

## Joining seams

Joining garment pieces together is known as finishing, and it also involves the weaving in of the loose ends. There are several ways to join seams together. Whichever method you use, make sure you do not pull the sewing up yarn too tight or your seams will pucker. If the garment is made with a very textured yarn, it is better to use a smooth yarn in a matching colour which will be easier to pull through the fabric.

**1** The most common, and probably the neatest method of joining two seams together, is mattress stitch. Place the pieces on a flat surface with right sides facing up. Thread a tapestry or blunt edged needle with matching yarn and begin by securing the yarn through both sides. Pick up the first stitch from one side but leave yarn loose (it will pull together every 3–4 stitches). Pick up the corresponding stitch on the same row on the other piece and sew back

and forth, picking up a stitch from each side. Make sure the yarn is tight enough to disappear, but not enough to shorten or pucker the seam.

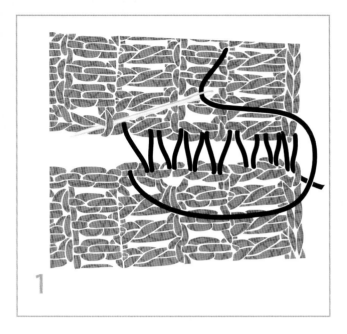

**2** Over sewing creates a slightly bulkier seam. Using matching yarn place right sides together and insert the needle back to front, sewing the two sides together with the yarn going over the edge. Insert the needle back to front again catching only one or two strands from each edge. Continue until the seam is finished.

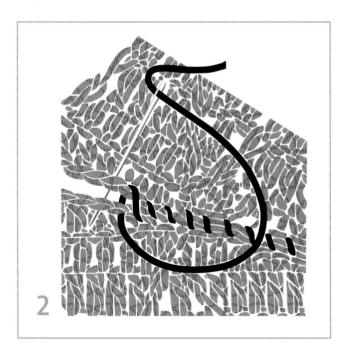

# Tension guide

Tension refers to how loose or tight you crochet your stitches. The recommended hook size on each pattern is the one used to work out the pattern and tension, and most crocheters will use this to achieve their own tension. However, it is the tension that is important and not the hook size.

Everyone crochets differently even when they are using the same yarn hook and pattern. Crochet a sample and keep changing the hook size until the sample is the same size as stated in the pattern. If you have too many stitches then go down a hook size; if you have too few then you will need to go up a hook size. You can also try wrapping the yarn around your fingers to control the tension by the way you feed the yarn to the hook. Either way you may need to practise a little to get the end result but it will be worth it in the end.

# Abbreviations

**ch** = **chain**

**sl** = **slip stitch**

**st** = **stitch**

**dc** = **double crochet**

**tr** = **treble**

**lp** = **loop**

# Glossary

## US/UK crochet terms and equivalents

| US | UK |
|---|---|
| chain (**ch**) | chain (**ch**) |
| single crochet (**sc**) | double crochet (**dc**) |
| double crochet (**dc**) | treble (**tr**) |
| half double crochet (**hdc**) | half treble (**htr**) |
| triple crochet (**trc**) | double treble (**dtr**) |
| slip stitch (**sl st**) | slip stitch (**sl st**) |

# Suppliers

## Adriafil S.r.l.

Via Coriano,
58–47900
Rimini
Italy
www.adriafil.com

## Angel yarns

77 North Street
Portslade
East Sussex
BN41 1DZ
United Kingdom
www.angelyarns.com

## Artesano Ltd

28 Mansfield Rd
Reading
Berkshire
RG1 6AJ
United Kingdom
www.artesano.co.uk

## Debbie Bliss

Designer Yarns Ltd
Unit 8–10 Newbridge Industrial
Estate
Pitt Street
Keighley
West Yorkshire
BD21 4PQ
United Kingdom
www.designeryarns.uk.com

## Lucy Neatby

Tradewind Knitwear Designs
45 Dorothea Drive
Dartmouth
NS
B2W 5X4
Canada
www.tradewindknits.com

## Rowan

Green Lane Mill
Holmfirth
HD9 2DX
United Kingdom
www.knitrowan.com

## Sirdar Spinning Ltd

Flanshaw Lane
Wakefield
West Yorkshire
WF2 9ND
United Kingdom
www.sirdar.co.uk

## Thomas B. Ramsden Bradford Limited

Netherfield Road
Guiseley
Leeds
LS20 9PD
United Kingdom
www.tbramsden.co.uk

# Acknowledgements

I am hugely grateful to the people who have helped me to get these patterns together for my first book.

To my editors Gerrie Purcell and Rachel Netherwood for their amazing support, understanding and patience in me being a hopeless slow poke since having our last baby. Your enthusiasm has driven me on.

To my wonderful husband Klyve, who encouraged and held my hand every step of the way, I couldn't have done this without him. To Charlie, Jamie, Cameron, Lucas and fluffy baby Lilianna, my lovely, funny brood of kids. You have all put up with extreme dippiness and cremated food for longer than I care to remember; thank you for making me smile every day and for helping me not to take myself too seriously.

To my mum Alice, sister Fiona and mum-in-law Maisie for all their warmth, love and help. My home kept running because of them. To my father Peter who is no longer with us but continues to inspire me daily.

To Tamsyn Christopher who read and checked it all and to my fabulous crochet helpers Kal Mistry, Tam Siebenhall and Zoe Ashton-Worsnop, who helped pattern check and make items super fast and so chirpily; thanks so much girls.

To my pals on our forum who have kept me laughing with their zany humour and sharp wit.

GMC Publications would like to thank the following for their help in creating this book:

Paskins Town House
www.paskins.co.uk
for providing the photoshoot location for the projects on pages 12, 19, 33, 41, 42, 54, 64, 80, 89, 90, 94
Paskins Town House
18/19 Charlotte Street
Brighton
BN2 1AG.

Pelham House
www.pelhamhouse.com
for providing the photoshoot location for the projects on pages 16, 22, 27, 30, 36, 46, 53, 57, 63, 67, 68, 72, 76
Pelham House
St Andrews Lane
Lewes
East Sussex
BN7 1UW.

Harriet Hoff for styling of projects on pages 16, 22, 27, 30, 36, 46, 53, 57, 63, 67, 68, 72, 76.

Jan Hansen for hair and make-up for projects on pages 16, 22, 27, 30, 36, 46, 53, 57, 63, 67, 68, 72, 76.

Models Eliza Nightingale at MOT Models and Indre Serpytyte.

Simon Rodway for the illustrations on pages 80, 83, 106–122.

# Index

To place an order, or to request a catalogue, contact:

**GMC Publications**

Castle Place, 166 High Street, Lewes, East Sussex, BN7 1XU United Kingdom

Tel: 01273 488005 Fax: 01273 402866

Website: www.thegmcgroup.com

Orders by credit card are accepted